A TO Z

MY BOOK OF ANIMALS

Become Shakespeare .com

First published in 2022 by
BecomeShakespeare.com

One Point Six Technologies Pvt Ltd.
119-123, 1st Floor, Building J2, B - Wing,
WadalaTruck Terminal, Wadala East, Mumbai,
Maharashtra, India, 400022.
T: +91 8080226699

ISBN - 978-93-5458-983-6

Dedication

This book is dedicated to my children Vishakha and Anmol as I have fulfilled my wishes and promises by writing for them though they are grown up now.

A

A is for the tiny Ant
The black, brown, and red in colour
Its bite causes everyone to flutter
It lives in the Anthills in a group
Loads of food it carries on the back
It all depends if her mood is on track

Activity with A

HELP THE ANT FIND ITS FOOD

FILL IN THE BLANKS

1.The Ant is of _____, _____and ___colour.

2.Ant carries its ____.

3.Ants live in_____.

4.It is not big it is_____.

5.The food is carried on its _____.

B

B is for the busy black Bee
It buzzes and sits on the flower we see
It sucks the nectar of the flower
It takes it to the hive on the tree
Where it will make honey day and night
It stings if someone steals it without fright

Activity with B

MATCH THE FOLLOWING

1. Nectar	Colour
2. Black	Hive
3. Home	Flower

COUNT THE BEES AND FLOWERS

BIG BEES

____

SMALL BEES

____

COUNT FLOWERS

BLUE __________

WHITE __________

RED __________

YELLOW __________

C

C is for the cunning Cat
It comes furry black, grey and white
It has a tail, and shiny eyes
It mews when hungry or troubled
It searches for a fish or a rat
Cat jumps and climbs being thin or fat

Activity with C

CIRCLE THE RIGHT

THE CAT IS OF

GREEN

GREY

YELLOW

BLUE

WHITE

BLACK

THE CAT EATS

LION

RAT

BAT

FISH

CAT

A CAT HAS

TAIL

HORNS

EYES

POUCH

FUR

D

D is for the barking Dog
It runs, plays and stays in a kennel
Milk and bones are its favourite
The master loves him day and night
White, black, brown or grey
It can easily smell its prey

Activity with D

COLOUR AND LIST ANY FIVE BODY PARTS OF DOG YOU SEE IN THE PICTURE

FIVE BODY PARTS OF DOG

1. ______________________________
2. ______________________________
3. ______________________________
4. ______________________________
5. ______________________________

E

E is for the huge Elephant
More of black and rarely white
With its trunk it trumpets
It runs and lives in the jungle
The mahout feeds it with green grass
Strong with two tusks and a tail of class

Activity with E

LET US JOIN

E E H N T

L P A

E is for __ __ __ __ __ __ __ __

WRITE THE NUMBER

1. TAIL ____________________
2. LEGS ____________________
3. EYES ____________________
4. TUSKS ____________________
5. TRUNK ____________________

COLOUR

F

F is for the colourful Fish
It swims around only in water
Big and small, long and short
It looks pretty in a glass pot
In river and pond round and round
The big fish eats the small around

Activity with F

OPPOSITES

BIG ______________________________

LONG ______________________________

FISH LIVES IN

1. ______________________________
2. ______________________________
3. ______________________________
4. ______________________________

COLOUR THE FISHES IN THE AQUARIUM

G

G is for the Goat
It has horns and a tiny tail
It can climb the hills without fail
It eats leaves from the garden
Milk and meat we get from it
While walking in herds it bleats

Activity with G

TICK THE RIGHT ANSWER

1. The Goat eats	Grass
	Meat
	Leaves
	Milk
2. The Goat has	Pouch
	Tail
	Eyes
	Horns
3. The Goat gives	Honey
	Milk
	Meat
	Wool

H

H is for the running Horse
Men women and children ride
For them it is a matter of pride
Black brown and sparkling white
The tail dangles as it neighs
It feeds mostly on grass and hay

Activity with H

COLOUR IT BLACK

FILL IN THE BLANKS

1. The Horse is eating ___ and ____.
2. It has ____ legs.
3. It has ___tail.
4. It has colours ____ ____ ____.
5. _____ _____ and _______ride on the horse.

I

I is for the Ibex
Out on the mountains of snow
In brown and grey hair all over
Thin in summer and thick winter undercoat
A wild goat with big horns
Eating shrubs, bushes and grasses.

Activity with I

WRITE THE WORDS THAT END WITH 'S'

1. ______________________

2. ______________________

3. ______________________

4. ______________________

5. ______________________

WRITE THE OPPOSITE WORD

1. Out ______________________

2. Thick ______________________

3. Summer ______________________

J

J is for the wild Jackal
In black or colour brown
With sharp teeth it hunts around
Killing small animals and birds
With long legs it runs very fast
They howl and bark in the night

Activity with J

WRITE YES OR NO

1.Jackal is grey in colour ________________.

2.Jackal is a pet animal ________________ .

3.Jackal lives in a house ________________.

4.Jackal runs very slowly ________________.

5.Jackal has horns ________________.

THE SOUND OF THE JACKAL IS –

1. ________________________________

2. ________________________________

THE JACKAL HUNTS WITH-

1. ________________________________

2. ________________________________

K

K is for the Kangaroo
It leaps around on hind legs
It carries its baby in the pouch
Flowers and leaves it loves to eat
It chortles or barks to greet
It is grey, red or brown in colour

Activity with K

COLOUR AND NAME THE BODY PARTS

1. ______________________________
2. ______________________________
3. ______________________________
4. ______________________________
5. ______________________________

L

L is for the Lion
The king of the jungle
This large and heavy lives in a cave
It roars to shake the jungle
With a coat of orange, golden or brown
It kills and eats all small animals around

Activity with L

DESCRIBE THE LION

WHICH ANIMALS WILL LION EAT? CIRCLE THEM

Tiger Goat Jackal

Elephant Rabbit

M

M is for the Monkey
Jumping from one tree to another
With a long tail and colour brown
Munching bananas and peanuts all around
Holding and hugging its puny tightly
Chattering in numbers plenty

Activity with M

FILL IN THE BLANKS

1. How many monkeys _____.

2. Monkeys are _______, _______, _______,

_______,_____.

3. Monkeys are eating______.

N

N is for the Nyala
A brown spiral-horned antelope
Male is a bull female is ewe
In the dense lowlands of South Africa
Some with spots others with stripes
Eating fruits, flowers, grass and twigs

Activity with N

WRITE THE OPPOSITES

1. MALE ______________________

   BULL ______________________

2. Nyala eats ______________________.

3. Nyala is of __________ colour.

4. They are found in ______________________.

5. Name any four-body parts

   1. ______________________
   2. ______________________
   3. ______________________
   4. ______________________

6. It is a spiral ______________________

______________________.

O

O is for the Orangutan
The huge mammal living in jungle
With colour red brown up on the tree
Eating eggs and honey sweet
Swinging with hands and feet long
It is like a friend to all

Activity with O

LEARN THE SPELLING

O__ A__G__T__N

__ __ __ __ __ __ __ __ __

PUT A CIRCLE ON THE RIGHT

FOOD

GRASS MEAT MILK EGG HONEY

HOME

JUNGLE CAVE KENNEL TREE WATER

COLOUR

GREEN RED BLUE BROWN GREY

WORDS ENDING WITH __ING

1. S ______________________________
2. L ______________________________
3. E ______________________________

P

P is for Panda
The cute harmless animal
Black and white in colour
Eating bamboo shoots and leaves
The Giant and the small in jungle
Climbing trees but do not fall

Activity with P

MATCH THE OPPOSITES

Black	Fall
Climb	Small
Giant	White

WHAT WILL THE PANDA EAT?

1. ______________________________
2. ______________________________

Q

Q is for Quokka
The happiest animal of the world
With a short tail, round ears and pouch
It climbs the shrubs and small trees
Sleeps in day and out at night
Brown in colour with eating only leaves

Activity with Q

LEARN THE SPELLING

Q FOR

Q __ O __ __ A

WRITE THE WORDS ENDING WITH 'S'

1. ______________________________
2. ______________________________
3. ______________________________
4. ______________________________
5. ______________________________

Quokka is the ____________________ animal of the world.

WHICH TWO ANIMALS HAVE A POUCH?

1. ______________________________
2. ______________________________

R

R is for the Rabbit
In brown, black and soft white fur
With long ears and a short tail
Looking at it is a pretty sight
It digs its burrow in the ground
Eating carrots all the way around

Activity with R

COLOUR OF RABBIT

1. ______________________
2. ______________________
3. ______________________
4. ______________________

COLOUR OF CARROT

1. ______________________
2. ______________________

NUMBER OF EARS

____

A RABBIT LIVES IN A

____

S

S is for Salamander
The poisonous lizard on ground and water
Is never harmful to men all around
In colour yellow,black and brown
It hides in the rocks never to be found
Eating happily worms and snails

Activity with S

FILL IN THE BLANKS

S is for the -__ __ __ __ __ __ __ __ __ __

S __ L __ M __ __ __ __ __

Its hiding place is __ __ __ __ __

CIRCLE THE RIGHT

1.It eats- **CHOCOLATES**

LEAVES

WORMS

FLOWERS

SNAILS

2. Its colour is- **YELLOW**

WHITE

GREEN

BROWN

BLUE

T

T is for Tiger
A big cat with black stripes
The orange brown fur looks nice
A long tail and sharp teeth
It hunts the animals and eats meat
For him a goat or cow is a treat

Activity with T

HELP THE ANT FIND ITS FOOD

1. T _ G _ R
   Repeat __ __ __ __ __

2. A Big __ __ __

3. Colour __ __ __ __ __,
   __ __ __ __ __
   __ __ __ __ __ __

4. Body Parts
   1. ______________________
   2. ______________________
   3. ______________________
   4. ______________________
   5. ______________________

5. It Eats

______________________ ______________________

U

U is for the Urial

It is a wild sheep from Asia

With two very big horns and beard

It is of brown red colour

It lives on mountains and plains

Men hunt it for meat and skin

Activity with U

Body parts **1.** ______________________________

2. ______________________________

Place _ _ _ _

Lives on _ _ _ _ _ _ _ _ _

and _ _ _ _ _.

Urial gives _ _ _ _ **and** _ _ _ _.

It is a _ _ _ _ **Sheep.**

It is _ _ _ _ _ _ _ _ **colour.**

URIAL

V

V is for Viper

A member of snake family

It lives in land and water

It hisses and comes in all shades of brown

Full of poison to kill a man

It eats the frogs and lizards around

Activity with V

TICK THE CORRECT

A VIPER EATS

Mango

Lizards

Potato

Frogs

A VIPER IS A

Bird

Fish

Snake

Dog

A VIPER LIVES IN

Sky

Land

Water

Mountains

A VIPER IS FULL OF

Milk

Water

Poison

Juice

W

W is for the Whale
The huge mammal in the ocean
It swims across with confidence
They eat all the small fish in the sea
The blue grey colour of the skin
No one can touch it even the kin

Activity with W

COLOUR THE FISHES

BLACK

BLUE

YELLOW

GREEN

X

X is for Xerus
A squirrel from Africa
A fluffy tail to hide from sun
Insects and seeds it eats with fun
Brown, red or white in colour
They live in groups in great number

Activity with X

LET US REVISE THE POEM

X is for the X __ __ __ __

A __ __ __ __ __ __ __ __ from __ __ __ __ __ __

A fluffy __ __ __ __ to hide from __ __ __

__ __ __ __ __ __ __ and __ __ __ __ __ it eats

for fun

__ __ __ __ __, __ __ __ or __ __ __ __ __ in

colour

They live in __ __ __ __ __ __ in great number.

Y

Y is for Yak

Up on the mountains black or brown
Four fat legs and body round
They eat the herbs and mosses all around
A long tail with two horns
It grunts and squeaks on the grassland

Activity with Y

COLOUR AND LABEL THE BODY PART

Z

Z is for Zebra

It lives on the grasslands of Africa
The white and black stripes bright
Grass, stem and leaves they eat day and night
They run in herds in the jungle
They kick and bite if troubled

Activity with Z

MATCH THE FOLLOWING

1. Colour	Africa
2. Home	Black
3. Food	Jungle
4. Country	Grass

COLOUR THE ZEBRA CROSSING

FUN WITH A TO Z

LET US LEARN A FEW SOUNDS

1.Bee ______________________________

2.Cat ______________________________

3.Dog ______________________________

4.Elephant __________________________

5.Goat ______________________________

6.Horse _____________________________

7.Jackal _____________________________

8.Kangaroo___________________________

9.Lion ______________________________

10.Monkey ___________________________

11.Nyala ____________________________

12.Viper ____________________________

WILD ANIMALS

1.Ant ___ ___ ___

2.Elephant ___ ___ ___ ___ ___ ___ ___ ___

3.Ibex ___ ___ ___ ___

4.Jackal ___ ___ ___ ___ ___ ___

5.Kangaroo ___ ___ ___ ___ ___ ___ ___ ___

6.Lion ___ ___ ___ ___

7.Monkey ___ ___ ___ ___ ___ ___

8.Nyala ___ ___ ___ ___ ___

9.Orangutan ___ ___ ___ ___ ___ ___ ___ ___ ___

10.Panda ___ ___ ___ ___ ___

11.Quokka ___ ___ ___ ___ ___ ___

12.Salamander___ ___ ___ ___ ___ ___ ___ ___ ___ ___

13.Tiger ___ ___ ___ ___ ___

14.Urial ___ ___ ___ ___ ___

15.Viper ___ ___ ___ ___ ___

16.Whale ___ ___ ___ ___ ___

17.Xerus ___ ___ ___ ___ ___

18.Zebra ___ ___ ___ ___ ___

THE JUNGLE STORY

LIST THE ANIMALS IN THE PICTURE

1. ______________________
2. ______________________
3. ______________________
4. ______________________
5. ______________________
6. ______________________
7. ______________________
8. ______________________
9. ______________________
10. ______________________